One day Kevin and Wellington were going along the path to the pond. Kevin left the path to sniff for rabbits in the long grass.

He saw a bent stick.

It had string on one end.

"Look, Wellington," he said.

"This is a fishing rod."

Wellington was sniffing in the long grass too.

He saw a long thin stick.

It had a net on one end.

"This is a fishing net," he said to Kevin. "Let's go fishing."

So the two dogs went to the pond to do some fishing.

They were sitting very still on the grassy bank .

Kevin was holding the fishing rod.

Wellington was holding the fishing net.

All of a sudden, Kevin felt something pull the string.
Then Wellington felt something pull the net.
Pull ... pull ... pull ... pull

Oh no! Kevin had a frog dripping from the string.

Oh no! Wellington had a frog dripping in the net.

"This is not fishing," said Kevin.

"This is catching frogs."

So the dogs let the frogs go, and they went back to the kennel.